Text copyright © 2021 by Harriet Ziefert
Illustrations copyright © 2002, 2021 by Emily Bolam
All rights reserved / CIP Data is available.
First published in the United States 2002 by
Blue Apple Books, South Orange, New Jersey
www.blueapplebooks.com

Does a Lion Brush?
Does a Pig Flush?

Harriet Ziefert

illustrations by
Emily Bolam

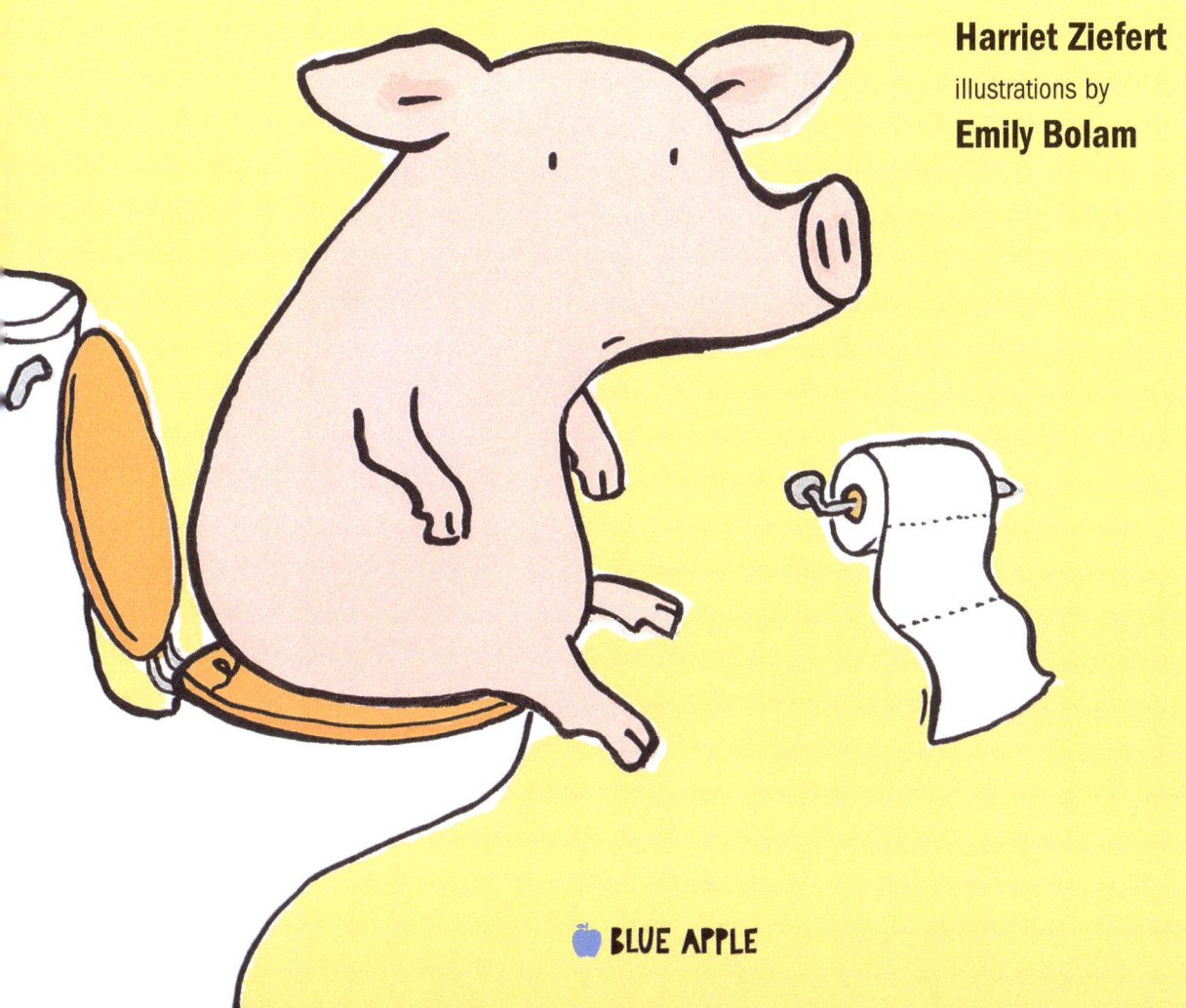

BLUE APPLE

PART 1
Flushing

Cow poop is called "flop."
After awhile, it becomes manure,
which is good for plants.

Fish poop while they're swimming—even while they're eating. Do you see the fish who's eating and pooping?

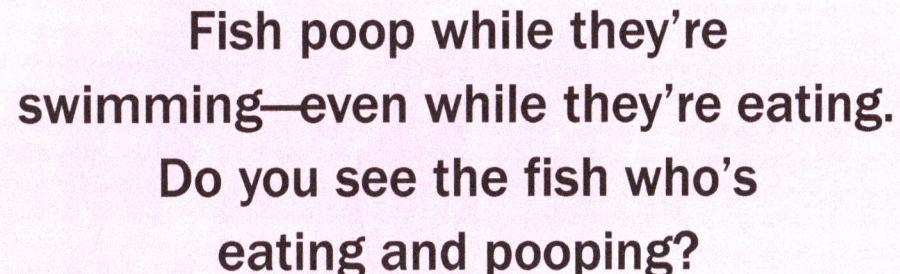

All animals poop. They poop to get rid of waste their bodies can't use. People train their dogs to poop outside.

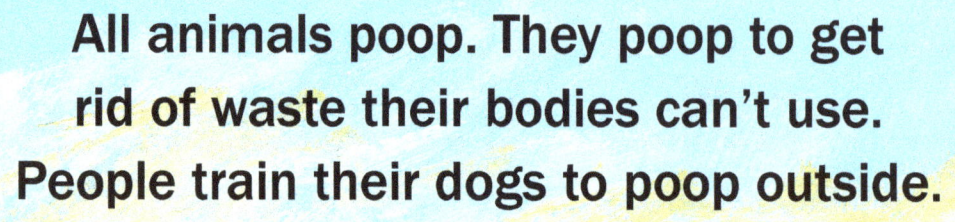

Cats can be trained to use litter boxes.

Neither dogs nor cats will poop where they sleep.

Then they say, "No more diapers.
It's time to use the toilet."

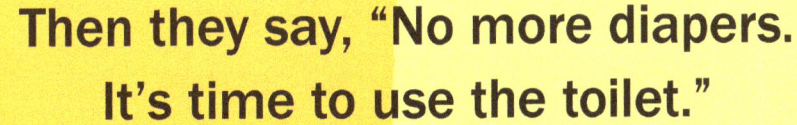

Zelda learns to pee and poop in the toilet.

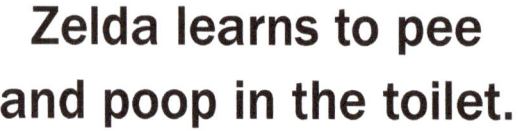

When she's done, she washes her hands with soap. Poop has germs, so it's important to wash your hands.

PART 2
Brushing

Does a lion brush its teeth?

**Oh, no!
Lions don't brush their teeth!**

Oh, no!
Bears don't brush their teeth!

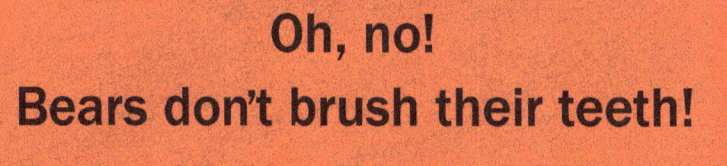

Does a penguin brush its teeth?

Animals clean their teeth
by chewing and gnawing.

But people do not.

Little kids brush.

Children have
20 baby teeth.

And they all need brushing.

It's important to brush your teeth after meals and before bedtime. Here's a good way to do it:

Put a small dab of toothpaste on your toothbrush.

Brush gently with short up-and-down and back-and-forth motions.

Brush just a couple of teeth at a time, on the outside, on the inside, and on the chewing surfaces.

Rinse and spit…
and try not to swallow any toothpaste.

www.ingramcontent.com/pod-product-compliance
Lightning Source LLC
LaVergne TN
LVHW070837080426
835510LV00026B/3420